REPORT TO THE PRESIDENT AND CONGRESS

DESIGNING A DIGITAL FUTURE: FEDERALLY FUNDED RESEARCH AND DEVELOPMENT IN NETWORK ING AND INFORMATION TECHNOLOGY

JANUARY 2013

The President's Council of Advisors on Science and Technology

Executive Summary

The impact of networking and information technology (NIT) is stunning. Virtually every human endeavor is affected as advances in NIT enable or improve domains such as scientific discovery, human health, education, the environment, national security, transportation, manufacturing, energy, governance, and entertainment. NIT is also a powerful engine for economic growth.

The United States leads the world in both the science of NIT and the myriad uses that transform lives. U.S. leadership stems from a sustained Federal investment in fundamental NIT research and development (R&D) spanning more than sixty years, and a vibrant industrial base that converts the fruits of that research to products. The research addresses both core NIT capabilities and the increasingly diverse domains in which NIT plays a crucial role. The interplay of Federally-funded university and government-agency research, privately funded industrial research, and entrepreneurial companies, together with the education and training that fuels innovation and productivity, clearly strengthens the Nation's prosperity, health, and security.

The role of NIT in meeting future challenges is even greater than in the recent past. NIT is now a fundamental part of U.S. infrastructure—for communication, for commerce, for defense, for education, for safety, and for quality-of-life. The nature of NIT continues to change rapidly, demanding continuing U.S. attention to the R&D that fuels that change. The challenges are far more multidisciplinary than before, increasing the importance of R&D that crosses agency boundaries as well as effective government coordination of its NIT R&D investments. More than ever, the future depends on strengthening U.S. NIT R&D capabilities.

The High-Performance Computing Act of 1991 established an R&D program in NIT, consisting of investments by multiple government agencies, a coordinating body within the government, and an advisory committee drawn from the academic and private sectors. The scope of the High-Performance Computing Act was expanded by the Next Generation Internet Research Act of 1998, and again by the America COMPETES Act of 2007. The term "NITRD" is now used to designate both the portfolio of government investments and the coordinating process. The National Coordinating Office (NCO) is responsible for managing the coordination process.[1] The President's Council of Advisors on Science and Technology (PCAST) has responsibility for the advising role.

In 2010, PCAST formed a Working Group that conducted a major review of the NITRD program, including both the portfolio of investments and the coordinating process.[2] Recommendations from the 2010 report are summarized in Appendix A. In 2012, PCAST asked a small Working Group to review progress

---

1. Earlier names for both "NITRD" and the NCO were changed as the scope of the program increased.
2. President's Council of Advisors on Science and Technology. (2010). "Designing a Digital Future: Federally Funded Research and Development in Networking and Information Technology", Report to the President and Congress. www.whitehouse.gov/sites/default/files/microsites/ostp/pcast-nitrd-report-2010.pdf.

since the 2010 report. The primary purpose of the 2012 review, described in this document, is to assess progress on the recommendations made in 2010 and make further recommendations in response to the activities and advances since 2010.

The 2012 Working Group found that in some areas of NIT R&D, there have been important investments that are responsive to the 2010 recommendations. In most of the areas that have received less attention and investment than was recommended, initial steps have been taken in some agencies, but interagency collaboration and synergy appears to be lacking. Specific analyses, findings, and recommendations appear in Section III of this report. In summary,

- Notable progress was identified in multi-agency investments in "big data," NIT-enabled interaction with the physical world, health IT, and cybersecurity. These areas remain as critical focal points in 2012 and beyond. Continued emphasis and even greater coordination is recommended.

- The area of social computing augments the study of individual human-computer interaction with research in social collaboration and problem-solving in a networked, online environment. Since 2010, several NITRD agencies have established independent research programs and initiatives in social computing. Now the need for cross-agency collaborative research in this area is even more crucial than before. Particularly for national priorities in energy, health, governance, and any area that may require the mobilization of citizen involvement, the ability to harness the possibilities in social computing is likely to grow in importance.

- Privacy and protected disclosure was cited as a cross-cutting theme in the 2010 report—one that is important for every agency and mission, as huge amounts of diverse information about individuals become available in online electronic form. However, no agency has primary responsibility for privacy R&D. Research on privacy is needed to inform policy decisions and to enable appropriate use of personal data while protecting its source. The urgency of this need cannot be overstated. Without clear scientific and engineering principles to rely on for guidance, policies and legislative actions may be taken that preclude progress or the exploitation of opportunities.

- Software technology is a challenge that cuts across every agency and thus, calls for interagency research coordination. Overall, while progress in software R&D appears to be good, it is hard to discern disruptive advances emerging out of the current programs. Software technology instead appears to be a domain of relentlessly incremental, albeit necessary, improvements to the state of the art. In order to sustain the Nation's capabilities, it is critical that such research be supported. At the same time, new concepts that may lead to greater advances must be sought.

- The 2010 NITRD report made two educational technology recommendations: (a) support for NIT R&D to discover new educational technologies applicable from pre-school settings all the way through life-long learning and (b) support for a long-term program to assess promising educational technologies and facilitate the evolution of curricula and instructional processes to incorporate them. There does not appear to have been progress on either of those collaborative activities. New educational technologies are emerging that create an opportunity to advance education and training. To date, the Federal Government is providing no coordination and inadequate R&D to take advantage of these opportunities.

- In the 2010 NITRD report, energy and transportation were called out as areas ripe for increased NIT R&D. Progress in the NIT issues recommended in the 2010 NITRD report appears to be modest. Multi-agency support is needed for NIT research to enable dynamic power management, achieve low-power systems and devices, and improve surface and air transportation, combining basic research with mission specific challenges.

- Significant progress has been made in creating infrastructure for network scaling and testbeds. Continuing attention has been paid to spectrum sharing and there have been some investments in basic research for spectrum management. Attention to other aspects of system scaling, such as robustness and resource management, is less evident.

- The 2010 NITRD report included an extensive discussion, a number of findings, and a specific recommendation related to Federally-funded R&D in the area of high-performance computing (HPC). There is still no coordinated, interagency plan for a substantial and sustained program of long-term, fundamental research on architectures, algorithms, and software for future generations of HPC systems. The need for such a program has not diminished.

The NITRD coordination effort is an effective mechanism for sharing information and coordinating activities that benefit multiple agencies. Under the NCO's guidance, coordination of cross-agency investments is managed by the NITRD Subcommittee, and by a collection of Interagency Working Groups (IWGs), Coordinating Groups (CGs), and Senior Steering Groups (SSGs). NITRD coordination is discussed in Section IV. In summary,

- The IWGs and CGs map to the Program Component Areas (PCAs) used to report NITRD elements of each Agency's budget. In this fast-moving discipline, the PCAs change very slowly. The 2010 report recommended that the structure of the IWGs/CGs be decoupled from the PCAs so that the coordinating function could keep up with changes in NIT, but that change was not made.

- In contrast, SSGs are not tied to budget reporting categories. Their members have higher rank in their organizations than IWG or CG members, and usually have some budget authority. The SSG mechanism allows for increased flexibility and timeliness in forming interagency groups addressing areas of national priority. One SSG existed at the time of the 2010 report, and four additional SSGs have been formed since then. SSGs are a significant and important addition to the NITRD coordination process; they engage in planning and coordination for important emerging areas that span agencies.

- As the impact and the innovative use of NIT have broadened, its importance affects agencies that have not been part of NITRD. Several additional agencies have joined NITRD since 2010, and a few others are participating in selected NITRD Groups. However, the Department of Education (DoEd) and several agencies with responsibility for aspects of health and healthcare are still missing.

- An area of concern in the 2010 report was the inability to fully quantify and properly categorize government investment in NIT R&D, so that future investment decisions could be informed by knowledge of current investment. A key finding of this review is that there are intrinsic barriers to obtaining transparent NIT R&D budget information, ranging from insufficient digitization of budgetary information, to a wide variety of reporting styles among government agencies, to a reluctance to classify budgeted expenditures as NITRD-related if they would increase the agency's contribution to NCO expenses. Yet, it remains crucial to understand whether the Federal Government's investment is adequate to meet present and future needs and whether important emerging areas are receiving enough funding.

Both the 2010 report and earlier portions of this document have emphasized the U.S. and world dependence on NIT, and the historical U.S. expertise and leadership in advancing NIT through a vibrant program of basic and applied research, a strong NIT industry, and a skilled workforce. The continued strength of U.S. expertise and leadership is crucial. Issues of government leadership are discussed in Section V. In summary,

- Both discovery and use of NIT advances require an NIT-educated community of innovators, workers, and citizens. That education must start in childhood and continue for a lifetime. There are promising signs of increased attention to NIT education and training, in terms of identifying curricula for K-12, training teachers, and educating adults to meet particular mission agency needs. Yet, progress is slow, and many children and adults are not well-equipped for the digital age. The states have been slow to introduce concepts of computer fluency in K-12.[3] Higher education is not keeping up with the projected increasing demand for employees in computing occupations.[4] Broader NIT education at all levels is essential.

- The path to the future depends on continuing strategic investments in a robust NIT R&D program. A balance must be struck between emerging and potentially transformative research and aspects of important core areas in which continued progress is essential. Determining a national strategy for R&D investment requires not only the dedication of people at the highest levels of government, but also sustained discipline-specific advice from leading experts in academia and the private sector. The 2010 PCAST NITRD report recommended the establishment of a broad high-level standing committee to provide this guidance. Since 2010, the need has only grown. We, therefore, recommend that PCAST itself form a standing subcommittee dedicated to this purpose, with an associated working group. The new working group would engage appropriate expertise from the NIT community and would operate on a regular and ongoing (as opposed to a project-specific) basis. The working group would survey the field and propose findings and recommendations, which PCAST could adopt in appropriate PCAST reports (including, but not limited to, the biennial NITRD program review). The standing subcommittee and working group we recommend would function in a manner analogous, in certain respects, to that of the very active and effective PCAST subcommittee and working group dedicated to advanced manufacturing.

---

3. ACM and Computer Science Teachers Association. (2010). "Running on Empty: The Failure to Teach K–12 Computer Science in the Digital Age." www.acm.org/runningonempty/fullreport.pdf, Fig. 8. Computer fluency is "a robust understanding of what is needed to use information technology effectively across a broad range of applications." It is a stronger notion than computer literacy, which implies competency with computer applications such as word processing and e-mail. The term was introduced in "Being Fluent with Information Technology," National Academies Press. (1999).

4. Department of Labor. (2012). Bureau of Labor Statistics 2010/2020 Employment Projections (Computing Occupations). www.bls.gov/emp/ep_table_102.htm, www.bls.gov/emp/ep_table_112.htm.

2012 PCAST Recommendations

Initiatives and Investments in NIT R&D to Achieve America's Priorities and Advance Key NIT Research Frontiers

Recommendation 1: Big data, NIT-enabled interaction with the physical world, health IT, and cybersecurity continue to be important, and while there is noticeable progress on interagency coordination since 2010, these areas remain as critical focal points in 2012 and beyond. Continued emphasis and even greater coordination is recommended.

Recommendation 2: The National Science and Technology Council (NSTC) should create a multi-agency collaborative effort, with the National Science Foundation (NSF) and Defense Advanced Research Project Agency (DARPA) as lead agencies, to develop a coordinated cross-agency initiative in social computing, building on the research results and understanding emerging from existing programs such as NSF's Social-Computational Systems Program (SoCS).

Recommendation 3: NSTC should create a multi-agency collaborative effort led by NSF, the Department of Health and Human Services (HHS), and DARPA to develop the scientific and engineering foundations of privacy R&D. NITRD should coordinate across government agencies to develop deployable technologies and inform policy decisions.

Recommendation 4: NSF, DARPA, and agencies that need software tailored to their missions must collaborate to support core research that advances design, development, modification, and maintenance of all varieties of software, incorporating reliability, robustness, security, and specialization for particular domains. Both sustained investment to achieve long-term research goals and focused research to address near-term challenges must be supported.

Recommendation 5: NSTC should create a multi-agency collaborative effort led by NSF and DoEd to define an R&D program with two major foci—to develop innovative educational technologies for learning from pre-school to life-long learning, and to develop assessment programs for those technologies that use advanced techniques from "big data" R&D and from the learning sciences. DoEd should join NITRD and should participate actively in this effort.

Recommendation 6: NSF, the Department of Energy (DoE), the Department of Defense (DoD), and the Department of Transportation (DoT) should collaborate to support research on the use of NIT for dynamic power management, for achieving low-power systems and devices, and for improving surface and air transportation, combining the basic research sponsored by NSF with the mission specific challenges faced by DoE, DoD, and DoT.

Recommendation 7: System and network scaling continues to be an important research challenge. NSF, and in the case of spectrum, the Federal Communication Commission (FCC) and the National Telecommunications and Information Administration (NTIA), should continue to invest in furthering these areas.

Recommendation 8: NSTC should lead an effort by NSF, DoE, DoD, member agencies of the Intelligence Community, and other relevant Federal agencies to design and implement a joint initiative for long-term, basic research aimed at developing fundamentally new approaches to high-performance computing.

Improved Effectiveness of NITRD Coordination

Recommendation 9: NSTC and the White House Office of Science and Technology Policy (OSTP) should strengthen the flexibility and responsiveness of the NITRD coordinating structure by continuing the use of Senior Steering Groups, by decoupling the Interagency Working Groups and Coordinating Groups from the budget reporting structure, and by regularly reviewing the Group portfolio with an eye towards disbanding those Groups that have outlived their usefulness and starting others that reflect major changes in NIT R&D areas.

Recommendation 10: The Office of Management and Budget (OMB) should continue its effort to digitize funding information and to enhance capabilities to create meaningful summary reports that cross agency boundaries.

Recommendation 11: OSTP, with guidance from PCAST, should develop a combination of quantitative and qualitative methods to assess the adequacy and appropriateness of government investments in NIT R&D.

Government Leadership

Recommendation 12: The NSTC must continue to lead in bringing about the education of more children and adults in NIT, both through the efforts of its Committee on Science, Technology, Engineering, and Mathematics (STEM) Education in multi-agency programs to provide workers with skills in topics of importance to national priorities and in the creation of opportunities for high-quality continuing education in NIT.

Recommendation 13: The Federal Government must lead in continuing to ensure that strong multi-agency R&D investments are made in NIT to address important national priorities. PCAST should establish a high-level standing PCAST NIT subcommittee and associated high-level PCAST NIT working group, composed of expert academic scientists, engineers, and industry leaders who can provide sustained strategic advice.

PCAST NITRD
Working Group

Co-Chairs

Susan L. Graham
Pehong Chen Distinguished Professor of Electrical Engineering and Computer Science Emerita
University of California, Berkeley

Peter Lee
Corporate Vice President
Microsoft Research, USA

David E. Shaw*
Chief Scientist, D.E. Shaw Research
Senior Research Fellow, Center for Computational Biology and Bioinformatics
Columbia University

Staff

Amber Hartman Scholz[5]
Acting Executive Director, PCAST

Knatokie Ford
AAAS Science and Technology Policy Fellow, PCAST

*Denotes PCAST Member

---

5. Note: Deborah Stine, PCAST's Executive Director, staffed this study until her departure in September 2012.

Table of Contents

I. Introduction

The breadth of impact of networking and information technology (NIT) is stunning. NIT affects health, national security, economic well-being, education, past, present, and future knowledge of the world, our transportation, uses of energy, and entertainment. Changes continue at a rapid pace. Recent years have seen the rise of massive open online courses (MOOCs), driverless cars, social networking, and the Curiosity robot that is currently exploring Mars. Because of talented people, the freedom to innovate, and the wise Federal investments that have been made in research and development in NIT, the United States has led the world in the science of NIT and in its myriad uses.

This report assesses the status and direction of the Federal Networking and Information Technology Research and Development (NITRD) Program. Responsibility for assessment of the NITRD program, originally assigned to the President's Information Technology Advisory Committee (PITAC) was transferred to the President's Council of Advisors on Science and Technology (PCAST) in 2005. A thorough review was last conducted in 2010.[6] This report provides an update to the 2010 review, assessing the responses to the 2010 recommendations, the changes in the NITRD program since 2010, and the newly emerging areas within NIT.

The phrase "NITRD Program" is used in two ways in practice and in this report.

1. As a description of the mechanism by which the Federal Government coordinates its unclassified research and development (R&D) investments in Networking and Information Technology (NIT).

2. As the name for the unclassified Federal NIT R&D portfolio itself.

The Federal Government's investment in NIT R&D dates from the birth of the field more than 60 years ago. As a coordination effort, though, NITRD had its genesis in the High-Performance Computing Act of 1991—"An Act to provide for a coordinated Federal program to ensure continued U.S. leadership in high-performance computing."[7] Its scope was broadened by the Next Generation Internet Research Act of 1998, and again by the America COMPETES Act of 2007.

To assist in this assessment, PCAST appointed an expert three-person Working Group, which consulted with more than 38 individuals and drew upon a number of recent studies and reports.

---

6. See footnote 2.
7. High-Performance Computing Act of 1991 [As Amended Through P.L. 110-69, Enacted August 9, 2007]. www.house.gov/legcoun/Comps/computin.pdf.

The Organization of this Report

Section II of this report briefly reviews the comprehensive and deep impact of NIT R&D on nearly all aspects of discovery, well-being, and economic prosperity today, providing additional data that builds on the more extensive discussion in the 2010 report. As a field of science and engineering, NIT is arguably unique in the breadth and rapidity of its increasing role in affecting lives, achieving priorities, and addressing challenges as a Nation. With this backdrop, Section III reviews the progress that has been made in responding to the 2010 recommended initiatives and investments in NIT R&D to achieve America's priorities and to advance key NIT research frontiers. This review has resulted in new findings, and in some cases, has led the committee to make new recommendations.

Looking to the future, effective coordination of the Nation's investments in NIT R&D is even more important than in the past. Section IV reviews the key role of the NITRD coordination process and the progress made in responding to the 2010 recommendations for improved effectiveness of NITRD coordination. Section V revisits the 2010 recommendations for government leadership in NIT R&D. The report concludes with a summary of where the NITRD program is now and where it needs to go in order to sustain America's leadership in NIT.

II. The Expanding Impact of Networking and Information Technology

A study recently published by the National Academies' Computer Science and Telecommunications Board (CSTB) asks the reader to imagine spending a day without NIT: [8]

This would be a day without the Internet and all that it enables. A day without diagnostic medical imaging. A day during which automobiles lacked electronic ignition, antilock brakes, and electronic stability control. A day without digital media—without wireless telephones, high-definition televisions, MP3 audio, cable- or Internet-delivered video, computer animation, and video games. A day during which aircraft could not fly, travelers had to navigate without benefit of the Global Positioning System (GPS), weather forecasters had no models, banks and merchants could not transfer funds electronically, and factory automation ceased to function. It would be a day in which the U.S. military lacked precision munitions, did not have the capabilities for network-centric warfare, and did not enjoy technological supremacy. It would be, for most people in the United States and the rest of the developed world, a "day the Earth stood still."

The breadth of impact of NIT is simply stunning. Virtually every human endeavor today is affected, as NIT enables or improves pursuits in domains as diverse as scientific discovery, human health, education, the environment, energy, national security, transportation, manufacturing, governance, and entertainment. In every case, discoveries and developments in NIT have enabled the United States to make major improvements and achieve progress towards national and global priorities. In the future many, if not most, of the new opportunities will be dependent on further advances in NIT.

The indispensable nature of NIT has made it the key technological driver for economic growth, and today, the economic impact of NIT continues unabated. According to a 2011 study by the McKinsey Global Institute, Internet-related activities alone contributed 3.8 percent to the U.S. gross domestic product (GDP) in 2009.[9] The Bureau of Economic Analysis estimates that "information-communications-technology-producing" industries contributed nearly 5 percent to overall U.S. GDP in 2010, an increase of over 16 percent from the previous year.[10]

The intellectual agenda of NIT research continues to expand, making possible new scientific discoveries and taking the research community into a multitude of new directions of scholarly inquiry. This culture of discovery has nourished a vibrant capacity for invention and innovation, which in turn has resulted in new business opportunities and a relentless growth in NIT-related industries. The study by the CSTB depicted this connection between intellectual vitality and economic impact in NIT industries through the use of a diagram, shown in Figure 1. This so-called "Tire Tracks" shows the rich interplay between

---

8. National Academies Press. (2012). Continuing Innovation in Information Technology. 1.

9. Matthieu Pélissié du Rausas, James Manyika, Eric Hazan, Jacques Bughin, Michael Chui, and Rémi Said. (2011). "Internet Matters: The Net's Sweeping Impact on Growth, Jobs, and Prosperity." McKinsey Global Institute, May, www.mckinsey.com/Insights/MGI/Research/Technology_and_Innovation/Internet_matters. The authors define "Internet-related activities" as the "totality of Internet activities (e.g., e-commerce) and . . . a portion of the information and communication technologies sector delineated by such activities, technologies, and services linked to the Web."

10. Bureau of Economic Analysis. (April 26, 2011). "2010 Recovery Widespread across Industries." www.bea. gov/newsreleases/industry/gdpindustry/2011/pdf/gdpind10_adv_fax.pdf. See also "Interactive Access to Industry Economic Accounts Data," www.bea.gov/iTable/iTable.cfm?ReqID=5&step=1.

Federally-funded research in both universities and industry. Each "track" starts at the bottom with Federally-funded basic NIT research. As time progresses, an ecosystem involving academia, industry, and government interacts in complex ways to create technological innovations that lead to entirely new product categories and, ultimately, to the creation of whole new industries. These NIT industries, each one sustaining annual revenues of over $10 billion (B), are arrayed along the tops of the tire tracks, along with a tiny sample of well-known companies and products as representatives of major economic impact. The links between government support, university research, and industrial R&D that are depicted in the figure reflect a remarkable and complex research ecosystem, on which future well-being will depend.

Figure 1. Tire Tracks Diagram

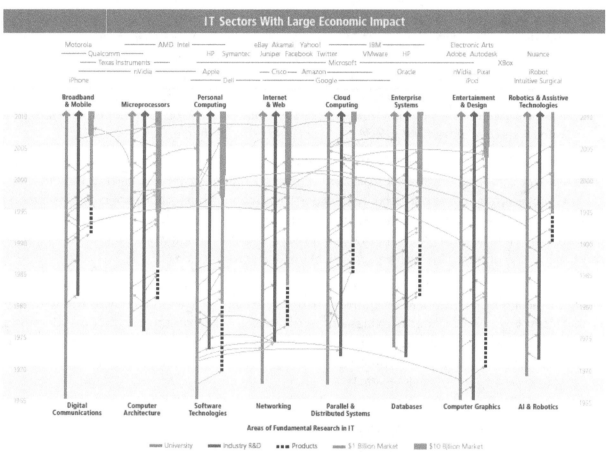

Even in just the two short years since the 2010 PCAST report on NITRD, advances in the understanding of the technical foundations of several key technical areas, such as "big data" and social computing have already enabled significant growth in emerging industry sectors, such as cloud computing and social networking. But this is just scratching the surface of the true opportunities.

Today, many of the grand challenges in NIT R&D are increasingly aligned with the Nation's priorities. Can robotics and other automated systems be created to reinvent core aspects of manufacturing and transportation systems, dramatically improving quality, safety, and energy efficiency? Can a secure, more robust, and more private Internet be created? Can more effective, personalized, and collaborative educational tools for universally available tutoring and just-in-time learning be created? Can more personalized and continuous health monitoring be developed? Can systems that enable people to engage with their governments and their communities more effectively be created? And can tools that accelerate discovery and innovation by enabling new forms of data-driven science and engineering be developed?

These and many other grand challenges are representative of a sea change in the thinking of the research community. To be sure, there is still a focus on the core research in basic understanding of the nature of computation and methods for harnessing it; but whole new vistas for real-world impact are opening, and both the research community and Federal agencies are showing eagerness to explore them.

While such opportunities are exciting, major obstacles loom. The classical distinction between "basic" and "applied" research hardly applies in NIT R&D. For example, initiatives in areas such as robotics or "big data" are cutting-edge fundamental research topics at universities and industry labs, while at the same time, they are the focus of real-world deployment missions for large corporations, the military, and government agencies. Whereas the intellectual challenges in NIT of the previous era were primarily in the development of NIT itself, the problems emerging today have a fundamentally different flavor, one that is far more multidisciplinary than before. Addressing the emerging challenges calls for a more collaborative approach, and in particular, collaborations that span the traditional domains of various Federal agencies. Achieving progress towards the national priorities in health, energy, manufacturing, education, and privacy will almost certainly depend on finding and exploiting synergies across multiple Federal agencies.

To this end, the 2010 PCAST report on NITRD recommended that steps be taken to develop an understanding of investment levels in NIT R&D, and then to create effective collaborations across key Federal agencies. As a result, much of the current review of the NITRD programs has centered on these dual issues of investment level and effective collaboration. To address those issues, a third area of focus for this review pertains to the advisory mechanism for meeting these NIT challenges. We address the question of whether an adequate high-level advisory mechanism exists, in light of the 2010 PCAST report's recommendation for a new standing committee, and propose revised recommendations based on our findings.

III. Progress in 2010 Recommended Initiatives in NIT R&D to Achieve America's Priorities and Advance Key NIT Research Frontiers

The primary focus of this review is the progress in responding to the recommendations made in the 2010 PCAST NITRD report. The 2010 report made a large number of recommendations for initiatives and investments in NIT R&D, both in the executive summary and, additionally, in the body of the report. The report recommended new initiatives in three areas, NIT for health, NIT for energy and transportation, and NIT for assuring both the security and the robustness of cyber-infrastructure. It recommended increased investment in fundamental NIT research frontiers and in key core technologies, including privacy and protected disclosure; social computing (including both the dynamics of online social systems and methods for harnessing large numbers of networked people and machines); data collection, storage, management, and automated large-scale analysis; and NIT and the physical world. It recommended sustained investment in research infrastructure and in important core NIT technologies, especially software creation, maintenance, and modification; scalable systems; and architectures, algorithms, and software for next-generation high-performance computing (HPC) systems. It recommended fundamental R&D to support educational technologies; infrastructure and tools for digital democracy; and a national infrastructure for spectrum management. Finally, it highlighted five major cross-cutting themes that impact virtually all Federal agencies—"big data," secure and trustworthy software systems, privacy and protected disclosure, interoperable and open interfaces, and supply chain vulnerability. The 2010 report advised that an investment of at least $1B annually would be needed for new, potentially transformative NIT research. The lack of clarity about current expenditures made it impossible to estimate how much of that would have to be new funding and how much could be obtained by reprioritization.

We first summarize those areas in which the response to the recommendations has been the strongest, and then discuss those areas in which progress has been slower.

Notable Areas of Progress in Responding to Recommendations

Big Data

Enormous volumes of data are now being generated from observational mechanisms (sensors, satellites, accelerators, telescopes, etc.), from computing simulations, and from social media (audio, visual, internet-based). Traditional textual documents (books, journals, newspapers, historical records) are increasingly available in digital form. With this rapid increase in data volume, new opportunities have arisen from fundamental NIT research, producing deep and sophisticated capabilities to analyze multi-faceted data, using modeling, data mining, and machine learning capabilities, and to glean a wide variety of information from that data. The topic that has come to be called "big data" augments those capabilities with fundamental research in data collection, storage, management, automated large-scale analysis of heterogeneous data, and widespread uses of the outcomes of that research. Data collection, storage, and management have been concerns for many years and have become increasingly challenging as the volume of data and diversity of data sources grows.

Virtually every government agency has growing needs for managing data and for the fruits of analysis. Recognizing that, the Office of Science and Technology Policy (OSTP) unveiled a "Big Data Initiative" in March 2012,[11] with $200 million (M) in new R&D investments. The new programs included a joint research solicitation from the National Science Foundation (NSF) and the National Institutes of Health (NIH), several basic research programs within NSF, a set of "Data to Decisions" programs from the Department of Defense (DoD), the Defense Advanced Research Project Agency (DARPA) XDATA project, NIH sharing of data from the 1000 Genomes Project, the Department of Energy (DoE) Scalable Data Management, Analysis and Visualization (SDAV) Institute, and a U.S. Geological Survey (USGS) program for "Big Data for Earth System Science." Several other agencies are contributing data sets to Data.gov. The NITRD coordination process introduced the Big Data Senior Steering Group (SSG) that will enable sharing of research projects and results that contribute to the missions of multiple agencies. All of these efforts strengthen the Nation's ability to address problems of national importance.

> **Finding:** Federal agencies have made significant progress in supporting R&D for data collection, storage, management, and automated large-scale analysis ("big data").

NIT-Enabled Interaction with the Physical World

Computer interaction with the physical world has a long history. Examples include industrial robots, robotic space explorers, and controllers embedded in appliances, automobiles, aircraft, and people. With the advent of wireless communication, device miniaturization, and better methods for computer vision, domain-specific sensor networks, wearable devices, new kinds of robotics, and a diversity of embedded smart devices have been advanced. Uses include healthcare, defense, basic research in physical and biological sciences, sustainability, public safety, manufacturing, and consumer goods and services.

The 2010 report viewed robotics and embedded systems as two related aspects of NIT interaction with the physical world, but in the government context they have remained largely separate. However, both aspects have made progress.

In June 2011, the President launched a National Robotics Initiative, to contribute to strengthening American manufacturing. This initiative focuses on developing robots that work with or beside people to extend or augment human capabilities, taking advantage of the different strengths of humans and robots. In addition to investing in the core technology needed for next-generation robotics, the initiative supports important applications of robotics. As part of that initiative, NSF, NIH, the National Aeronautics and Space Administration (NASA), and the U.S. Department of Agriculture (USDA) announced a joint research solicitation, with anticipated funding of $40-50M per year. DoD introduced a $40M Defense University Research Instrumentation Program. The National Robotics Initiative represents a response to emerging opportunities identified by the research community, effectively coordinating the activities and programs across multiple Federal agencies.

---

11. Office of Science and Technology Policy (OSTP) Press Release. (March 29, 2012). "Obama Administration Unveils 'Big Data' Initiative: Announces $200 Million in New R&D Investments." www.whitehouse.gov/sites/default/files/microsites/ostp/big_data_press_release.pdf.

Research in embedded systems has been coordinated through the High Confidence Software and Systems (HCSS) CG. More recently, that area has expanded to a new subfield of NIT called "cyber-physical systems" which incorporates sensors and sensor networks. The Cyber-Physical Systems Senior Steering Group (SSG) was formed in 2012. NSF, the National Institute of Standards and Technology (NIST), NASA, DoD, the National Oceanic and Atmospheric Administration (NOAA), the Environmental Protection Agency (EPA), DARPA, and the USGS have programs in aspects of cyber-physical systems. In this regard, the introduction and coordination of research initiatives across a large number of relevant agencies has been strong, likely creating the conditions for synergy as new funding programs are established.

> **Finding:** Federal agencies have made significant progress in supporting R&D for robotics and are continuing to create a coordinated response while also establishing new programs to fund advances in cyber-physical systems.

Health IT

NIT is playing an increasingly important role in all aspects of health and healthcare. There is tremendous potential in the use of NIT to accelerate progress in the fundamental technologies and delivery mechanisms for health and well-being. The possibilities include new capabilities in medical devices, data-driven development and discovery of new drug therapies, secure and robustly available health records, and personal responsibility for health maintenance. The potential to use data mining and machine learning on health and healthcare information about millions or even billions of people while protecting their privacy holds out the promise of applying collective experience and deep analysis for highly personalized health monitoring and treatment.

Although there has not been an overall government initiative on NIT for health, there has been a considerable amount of progress by multiple government agencies in response to both the 2010 PCAST NITRD report and the 2010 PCAST report on Health IT.[12]

The HHS Office of the National Coordinator for Health Information Technology (ONC), with multi-agency participation, funded four highly collaborative research projects under the Strategic Health IT Advanced Research Projects (SHARP) program. (Unfortunately, that program is ending and has no successor). NSF initiated the Smart Health and Wellbeing Program. Several institutes within NIH have NIT programs that go beyond electronic health records. There are also health IT projects within the Big Data Initiative for both data collection and data analytics and within the National Robotics Initiative for both surgery and prosthesis.

There are encouraging signs of progress in interagency collaboration. In response to the American Recovery and Reinvestment Act of 2009, the NCO established the Health Information Technology Research and Development (HITRD) SSG and the Health Information Technology Innovation and Development Environments (HITIDE) Subgroup to coordinate agency activities. The SSG has developed a report, "Federal Health IT R&D Recommendations," which is under review by OSTP. The HITIDE Subgroup is

---

12. President's Council of Advisors on Science and Technology. (2010). "Realizing the Full Potential of Health Information Technology to Improve Healthcare for Americans: The Path Forward." Report to the President and Congress. www.whitehouse.gov/sites/default/files/microsites/ostp/pcast-health-it-report.pdf.

working on plans for federated national testbeds for developing interoperable health records and health systems. The Veterans Health Administration (VHA) is participating in that Subgroup. It is anticipated that NSF and NIH will announce a joint research solicitation later this year.

Much research remains to be done. Many innovative ideas for personal health (approaches to empower individuals to sustain their own health and that of their families) are being explored, but research is needed to understand which are most effective and how they might evolve. There is a continuing need for testbeds, data sets, and platforms for strengthening research prototypes so they can be evaluated and improved at scale. Shared and open standards are needed for information exchange, so that multiple capabilities can be combined to solve complex problems.

> **Finding:** Federal agencies have made significant progress in supporting R&D for health IT and in increasing interagency collaboration.

Cybersecurity

The 2010 NITRD report identified cybersecurity as an area of great and growing importance. The report drew special attention to its implications for protecting the Nation's critical infrastructure, including civil and governmental communications networks, electrical power generation and distribution systems, financial systems, logistics, fuels, water, and emergency services. The report found that effectively defending cyber-infrastructure against potential adversaries, whose offensive capabilities are likely to grow significantly over time, will require the adoption of entirely new approaches, and will require a significant and ongoing investment in long-term, fundamental research in various areas of computer science.

There is now an increased awareness of the Nation's dependence on cyber-infrastructure and applications, and of the importance of improving the security of that infrastructure. NITRD has long had a Cyber Security and Information Assurance (CSIA) Interagency Working Group (IWG), and in 2008 created a higher-level CSIA R&D SSG. These two groups, along with the Special Cyber Operations Research and Engineering (SCORE) IWG (which addresses classified cybersecurity issues and R&D), provide coordination of Federal cybersecurity R&D.

The coordination structure is regarded as particularly effective. The CSIA IWG and SSG produced a report, *Trustworthy Cyberspace: Strategic Plan for the Federal Cybersecurity Research and Development Program*, which is very well regarded. Some of the people interviewed for this report, however, believe that the research itself is not well enough coordinated. It has been suggested that DoD, the National Security Agency (NSA), and the Department of Homeland Security (DHS) should pose unclassified challenges whose solutions advance the state of the art in ways that might help the U.S. intelligence community to address classified problems.

Investment in cybersecurity R&D has increased in recent years. NSF, DoE, DoD, and DHS all fund R&D programs on various aspects of cybersecurity, although there appear to be no joint programs. Supply chain risk management for NIT is being addressed by NIST in partnership with DHS. DoD is also concerned with supply chain risk; DoD and NSA have supported the Trusted Foundry Program since 2004.

One area deserving of more attention relates to the recommendation in the 2010 report for fundamental research in NIT-related areas relevant to the implementation of what was referred to in the report as a "survivable core" of essential cyber-infrastructure. The term "survivable core" was used in that context to refer to a small, rigorously isolated set of very basic capabilities that could be relied upon with a high degree of confidence to provide truly essential NIT-based services on a temporary basis in the event that, for example, a catastrophically damaging cyber-attack cannot be prevented. From a technical viewpoint, this is quite different from the problem of defending the highly complex systems used under non-emergent conditions, and its solutions are likely to require advances in different areas of NIT research.

Finding: Federal agencies have made substantial progress in supporting R&D for reducing the risks associated with various forms of cyber-attack, although much remains to be done.

Recommendation 1: Big data, NIT-enabled interaction with the physical world, health IT, and cybersecurity continue to be important, and while there is noticeable progress on interagency coordination since 2010, these areas remain as critical focal points in 2012 and beyond. Continued emphasis and even greater coordination is recommended.

Areas in Which Response to Recommendations Has Lagged

Social Computing

Use of the Internet by means of the World Wide Web has become universal and commonplace. Most of the content available to search engines is provided by users. Users collaborate informally by using services, such as Facebook and Twitter (both social media), and more intentionally, through enterprises, such as Wikipedia (an example of peer production). There is a growing phenomenon of "social computing," incorporating not only social media and peer production, but also crowdsourcing and collective distributed tasks. Recent examples include the DARPA Network Challenge, which demonstrated the ability of social networks to mobilize large numbers of people rapidly for the purpose of finding hidden red weather balloons, and the ReCaptcha system for human computation, to obtain accurate character recognition of scanned texts.

The 2010 NITRD report recommended that NSF, DARPA, and HHS create a collaborative research program that augments the study of individual human-computer interaction with research in social collaboration and problem-solving in a networked, online environment. Collective human-NIT interaction is a reality, with many examples of novel ways in which the problem-solving power of large numbers of network-connected people and machines can be used to great effectiveness. It is important that both the productive uses of this phenomenon and the problems it raises be understood.

All three agencies have expressed strong interest in this area. NIH is beginning to look at the use of social networking for health, and DARPA has identified social computing systems as one of the core areas for future programs. Social computing systems may enable disruptive advances in what kinds of problems can be solved, as well as provide a tool for mass mobilization and information dissemination in times of crisis. At NSF, the program in Social-Computational Systems (SoCS) seeks to develop greater coherence and "understanding about the properties that systems of people and computers together possess," leading to a concept of "socially intelligent computing." There are also some nascent studies of the use of social interaction for education, and NSF's Interface between Computer Science and Economics & Social Sciences (ICES) program is a multidisciplinary effort spanning three directorates.

While the above are important and useful starts on this emerging area, there still appears to be no focused effort spanning the three agencies to understand the technical effects on specific areas, such as security, privacy, health, and scientific discovery, from the emerging social phenomena that are empowered by ubiquitous online services.

> **Finding:** Several NITRD agencies and departments, including NSF, DARPA, and HHS, have established largely independent research programs and initiatives in social computing and areas directly relevant to social computing. These programs have started to identify the key research challenges and to develop a coherent taxonomy of this subfield of NIT R&D. Two years later, need for cross-agency collaborative research in this area is even more crucial. Particularly for national priorities in energy, health, governance, and any area that may require large-scale citizen involvement, the ability to harness the possibilities in social computing is likely to grow in importance.
>
> **Recommendation 2:** The National Science and Technology Council (NSTC) should create a multi-agency collaborative effort, with NSF and DARPA as lead agencies, to develop a coordinated cross-agency initiative in social computing, building on the research results and understanding emerging from existing programs, such as NSF's Social-Computational Systems Program (SoCS).

Privacy

Privacy and protected disclosure was cited as a cross-cutting theme in the 2010 report—one that is important for every agency and mission—as huge amounts of diverse information about individuals become available in online electronic form. The report said:

> *"Privacy challenges do not and must not require us to forgo the benefits of NIT in addressing national priorities. Rather, we need a practical science of privacy protection, based on fundamental advances in NIT, to provide us with tools we can use to reconcile privacy with progress."*[13]

Even ahead of the development and adoption of tools, science principles of privacy protection could do much to guide the development of more effective policies in this area.

There continues to be no focused coordinated R&D effort in privacy. Important issues to be addressed include how to realize the benefits of collective personal information without compromising the privacy of individuals, how to achieve cybersecurity and security more broadly without unnecessary disclosure of individual information, how to design systems to avoid unintended personal disclosure, how to empower individuals to assert their identity and also make informed decisions about voluntary disclosure, and how to use the science of privacy protection to inform policy decisions.

No mission agency has primary responsibility for privacy and protected disclosure—the issue arises as a byproduct of missions, such as health, defense, energy conservation, education, economic prosperity,

---

13. See footnote 2.

and others. Consequently, it appears that a coordinated NITRD effort driven in a non-partisan manner by the highest levels of government is needed to make progress on this topic.

The R&D challenge posed to the NITRD program by privacy is daunting. The technical foundations of privacy technologies and policies are likely to be technically complex, requiring results from deep research and a comprehensive, end-to-end view of the engineering and deployment issues. It is unlikely that any individual agency, on its own, can reach practical deployable solutions; effective collaboration will be essential. At the same time, it may be important for one agency to take the primary responsibility for privacy R&D, and then drive the necessary collaboration from there.

The urgency of this need cannot be overstated. Without clear scientific and engineering principles to rely on for guidance, policies and legislative actions may be taken that preclude progress or the exploitation of opportunities in the mission areas mentioned above.

> **Finding:** No agency has primary responsibility for privacy R&D, although many agencies need a better understanding of the science of privacy and protected disclosure in an online digital world. Research on privacy is needed to inform policy decisions and to enable appropriate use of personal data while protecting its source.
>
> **Recommendation 3:** NSTC should create a multi-agency collaborative effort led by NSF, HHS, and DARPA to develop the scientific and engineering foundations of privacy R&D. NITRD should coordinate across government agencies to develop deployable technologies and inform policy decisions.

Software

The problem of predictable development of software that has the intended functionality and is reliable, secure, and efficient remains as one of the most important problems in NIT. Software technology is a challenge that cuts across every agency and thus, calls for interagency research coordination. At the same time, the approaches to software development can vary significantly for emerging areas like "big data," robotics and physical systems, embedded systems, high-performance computing, and so on, expanding the challenges substantially. Furthermore, the evolution of computing infrastructure is creating new challenges, ranging from energy-aware software development to software for massively parallel and distributed systems.

Overall, while progress in software R&D appears to be good, it is hard to discern disruptive advances emerging out of the current programs. Software technology, instead, appears to be a domain of relentlessly incremental, albeit necessary, improvements to the state-of-the-art. In order to sustain the Nation's capabilities, it is critical that such research be supported. At the same time, new concepts that may lead to fundamental advances must be sought.

Sustained efforts must be supported for foundational advances in a full range of software technologies, including new languages for new domains, such as "big data" and embedded applications, tools for large-scale analysis and verification, and new approaches for easier development of software that exploit parallelism and heterogeneity.

> **Finding:** Software technology remains one of the most critical areas in NIT R&D, and while progress has been good on current foundations, the needed disruptive advances do not appear imminent.
>
> **Recommendation 4:** NSF, DARPA, and agencies that need software tailored to their missions must collaborate to support core research that advances design, development, modification, and maintenance of all varieties of software, incorporating reliability, robustness, security, and specialization for particular domains. Both sustained investment to achieve long-term research goals and focused research to address near-term challenges must be supported.

Educational Technology

The 2010 NITRD report made two recommendations concerning educational technology. The first was that the DoEd and NSF should support NIT R&D to discover new educational technologies applicable from pre-school settings all the way through life-long learning. The second was that the same two agencies should have a long-term program to assess promising educational technologies, and to facilitate the evolution of curricula and instructional processes to incorporate proven educational technologies. Neither of those collaborations appears to have made progress.

There has been a significantly increased deployment of educational technologies in the last two years. For example, the private sector has introduced a multiplicity of tablet based "apps" for education. College-level MOOCs have taken off, enabled by new technologies, such as auto-grading and online social collaboration, and new instructional approaches, such as small modular lessons and frequent automated quizzes to assess comprehension. There is an increasing interest in the use of electronic games to motivate and engage learners. The popularity of these technologies is apparent, but their efficacy is not well understood.

Assessment of the use of technology for education at all levels still needs research; there is still a preponderance of polling over objective analysis. The availability of digital data about the learning activities of users of educational technologies provides a new opportunity to create a more grounded assessment capability. That, in turn, would inform a more scientific basis for the creation of new personalized learning technologies. Although DoEd bears primary responsibility for K-12 education, other mission agencies, such as DoD, have a need for continuing education of their adult personnel. The Nation needs advances in education and training at all levels.

There are some scattered but promising activities in educational technologies. DoEd has an Office of Educational Technology that has ongoing programs using technology for children and adults with disabilities. DARPA sponsors the ENGAGE program to develop game-based programs for education. The Advanced Research Projects Agency for Education (ARPA-ED) program proposed in the 2010 PCAST education report would also fulfill some of these needs but to date it has not been established.

Finding: New educational technologies are emerging that provide an opportunity to advance education and training. To date, the government is providing no coordination and inadequate R&D to take advantage of these opportunities.

Recommendation 5: NSTC should create a multi-agency collaborative effort led by NSF and DoEd to define an R&D program with two major foci—to develop innovative educational technologies for learning from pre-school to life-long learning, and to develop assessment programs for those technologies that use advanced techniques from "big data" R&D and from the learning sciences. DoEd should join NITRD and should participate actively in this effort.

Energy and Transportation

In the 2010 NITRD report, energy and transportation were identified as areas ripe for progress by the introduction of NIT R&D. The 2010 recommendation stated:

"The Federal Government should invest in a national, long-term, multi-agency, multi-faceted research initiative on NIT for energy and transportation. As part of that initiative:

- DoE and NSF should be major sponsors of research for achieving dynamic power management in applications ranging from single devices to buildings to the power grid.

- NIST should organize the multi-stakeholder formulation of interoperable standards for real-time control. Interoperability facilitates repeated cycles of innovation by multiple vendors, promoting the development of versatile and robust NIT.

- DoD should continue to be a major sponsor of research on using NIT to achieve low-power systems and devices.

- The Department of Transportation (DoT) should sponsor ambitious NIT research relevant to surface and air transportation."[14]

Since the 2010 report, DoT has joined the NITRD program. NSF funds some aspects of energy research through its Science, Engineering, and Education for Sustainability (SEES) program. However, no initiative of the kind recommended has been created, and we have not found evidence of increased attention to NIT research in energy and transportation.

Finding: Progress in addressing the NIT issues recommended in the 2010 NITRD report appears to be modest.

Recommendation 6: NSF, DoE, DoD, and DoT should collaborate to support research on the use of NIT for dynamic power management, for achieving low-power systems and devices, and for improving surface and air transportation, combining the basic research sponsored by NSF with the mission specific challenges faced by DoE, DoD, and DoT.

---

14. See footnote 2.

Scalable Systems and Networking

As the 2010 NITRD report recommended, there has been continuing progress in scalable systems and networking. NSF has supported two networking infrastructure and scaling efforts, the Global Environment for Network Innovations (GENI), a virtual laboratory for at-scale networking experimentation, and US Ignite, a national-state, public-private partnership to foster the creation of novel applications and digital experiences that will transform healthcare, education and job skills training, public safety, energy, and advanced manufacturing. DoE continues to fund the Energy Sciences Network (ESnet) infrastructure to connect DoE laboratories and other research institutions. DoD continues to fund the Defense Research and Engineering Network (DREN) infrastructure to connect DoD laboratories and other research institutions for high-performance applications.

The 2010 NITRD report recommended that NSF, the Federal Communications Commission (FCC), and the National Telecommunications and Information Administration (NTIA) partner to create, sustain, and promote the use of a nationwide infrastructure for spectrum monitoring that cuts across commercial, public safety, and DoD applications. That recommendation was followed by a July 2012 PCAST report, "Realizing the Full Potential of Government-Held Spectrum to Spur Economic Growth,"[15] that explores the topic in considerably more depth. NTIA has set up a Spectrum Sharing Innovation Test-Bed Pilot Program to examine the feasibility of increased sharing between Federal and non-Federal users. NSF issued the "Enhancing Access to Radio Spectrum (EARS)" solicitation in FY12 "to identify bold new concepts with the potential to contribute to significant improvements in the efficiency of radio spectrum utilization, and in the ability for traditionally underserved Americans to benefit from current and future wireless-enabled goods and services."[16] The solicitation will be funded at $11M in FY12 and $50M in FY13.

Finding: There has been significant progress in creating infrastructure for network scaling and testbeds and continuing attention to spectrum sharing. There have been some investments in basic research for spectrum management. Attention to other kinds of system scaling, such as robustness and resource management, is less evident.

Recommendation 7: System and network scaling continues to be an important research challenge. NSF, and in the case of spectrum, FCC and NTIA, should continue to invest in furthering these areas.

High-Performance Computing

The 2010 NITRD report included an extensive discussion, a number of findings, and a specific recommendation related to Federally-funded research and development in the area of HPC.[17] Because the HPC-related recommendation was not highlighted within the executive summary, however, some readers failed to find it, and others inferred that PCAST believed HPC R&D was no longer important. In reality, the report placed a high priority on ambitious, long-term basic research aimed at developing

---

15. President's Council of Advisors on Science and Technology. (2012). "Realizing the Full Potential of Government-Held Spectrum to Spur Economic Growth." Report to the President and Congress. www.whitehouse.gov/sites/default/files/microsites/ostp/pcast_spectrum_report_final_july_20_2012.pdf.

16. National Science Foundation. (2012). Enhancing Access to the Radio Spectrum (EARS). www.nsf.gov/funding/pgm_summ.jsp?pims_id=503480&org=AST&from=home.

17. See footnote 2. xiii–xiv, Sections 6.7 and 7.

"truly transformational next-generation HPC systems," and called for a highly aggressive, coordinated program of "fundamental research on hardware, architectures, algorithms, and software with the potential for enabling game-changing advances in high-performance computing."

HPC differs from many other areas of NIT in that the government not only supports basic R&D in HPC, but is also the main consumer of the most powerful and expensive HPC systems. Various mission-oriented agencies within the DoE, the DoD, and the U.S. Intelligence Community rely on such systems to support their respective missions, as do a number of other Federal agencies. While HPC technologies have had a significant impact within the private sector as well, advanced HPC infrastructure is critical to national security, scientific discovery, and technological innovation, and substantial Federal funding must continue to be provided for its acquisition.

As noted in the 2010 report, however, it is important that the United States balances investments in present and future requirements for high-performance computing, and that procurement of current-generation machines does not "crowd out" the fundamental research in computer science and engineering that will be required to develop next-generation HPC technologies. To lay the groundwork for such next-generation systems, it will be necessary to pursue entirely new approaches, conducting groundbreaking research (including high-risk, high-return exploratory efforts) in a number of areas.

While the metric that has most commonly been used over the years as a proxy for high-end supercomputer performance is the number of floating point operations per second (FLOPS) executed on a specific numerical benchmark application, the sort of research program envisioned in the 2010 report would have a broader set of goals. In the context of an expanding and evolving set of national priorities, the report concluded that the notion of "high performance" must now assume a broader meaning, encompassing not only FLOPS, but also the ability, for example, to efficiently manipulate vast and rapidly increasing quantities of both numerical and non-numerical data, to handle problems requiring real-time response, and to accelerate many applications that were either non-existent or far less important at the time of NITRD's creation. With the advent of inexpensive multicore processor chips, powerful graphics processing units, cloud-based computational resources based on enormous numbers of processors, and other technological and commercial innovations, the report also recommended that the Nation's high-performance computing goals be coordinated with a qualitatively new and rapidly evolving "computational ecology."

The specific recommendation in the 2010 report was that a coordinated program be initiated to conduct basic research on architectures, algorithms, and software for next-generation HPC systems. As noted in the 2010 report, such a program could ultimately allow the United States to "leapfrog" other nations, maintaining the leadership position that America has historically enjoyed in high performance computing. So far as we have been able to determine, however, little progress has been made since the 2010 report on the implementation of such a program.

Finding: There is still no coordinated, interagency plan for a substantial and sustained program of long-term, fundamental research on architectures, algorithms, and software for future generations of HPC systems.

Recommendation 8: NSTC should lead an effort by NSF, DoE, DoD, member agencies of the Intelligence Community, and other relevant Federal agencies to design and implement a joint initiative for long-term, basic research aimed at developing fundamentally new approaches to high-performance computing.

Large-Scale NIT Infrastructure for Research and Development

Although the last two letters of the NITRD acronym might suggest otherwise, the NITRD program encompasses both NIT R&D and large-scale NIT-based research infrastructure investments. Large scale shared infrastructure includes not only HPC systems, but also networks used for experimentation, shared data bases, and shared open platforms that enable experimental replacement of components. Both research and the infrastructure to conduct research are important, and a balance in investment must be achieved. That balance can be challenging in times of flat budgets.

The manner in which investments are aggregated and reported in the Federal Government in some cases tends to obscure the distinction between (a) R&D in NIT disciplines, and (b) the acquisition of NIT infrastructure used to conduct R&D in other areas. The investment in NIT-based infrastructure for non-NIT research is more properly attributed to the domain in which it is used. Misclassifying infrastructure expenditures as R&D expenditures may lead policymakers to believe that the government is investing far more in the latter than is actually the case. This may lead to a systematic underinvestment in fundamental NIT research of the sort that will be required to preserve the Nation's historical leadership in NIT over future years.

IV. Progress in 2010 Recommendations for Improved Effectiveness of NITRD Coordination

Many Federal employees volunteer their time and energy to provide sustained leadership for the NITRD Program through its Subcommittee, its Interagency Working Groups (IWGs), its Coordinating Groups (CGs), and, more recently, its Senior Steering Groups (SSGs). This effort is recognized across the executive and legislative branches of the government as an effective mechanism for sharing information and coordinating activities of benefit to multiple agencies.

The recommendations in the 2010 report for improvements to NITRD effectiveness had two major thrusts—improving the effectiveness of NITRD coordination by varying its coordination structure and by increasing the membership of Federal agencies in NITRD and NITRD coordination, and improving the transparency of budgetary reporting. In both thrusts, there have been significant areas of progress, although in some aspects, progress has been less apparent.

Interagency Working Groups, Coordinating Groups, and Senior Steering Groups

The NITRD IWGs and CGs map to the Program Component Areas (PCAs) used to report NITRD elements of each agency's budget. In 2001, six of the seven IWGs/CGs were created and the High End Computing (HEC) PCA was divided into two: HEC-I&A (infrastructure and applications), and HEC-R&D. In 2005, the Cyber Security and Information Assurance (CSIA) PCA and an associated IWG were created. Thus, despite the many changes to NIT in the last decade or more, the structure of the PCA budget categories and the IWGs/ CGs has not changed very much. The NCO has argued that it is desirable to keep the PCAs unchanged in order to be able to do multi-year funding comparisons. The 2010 PCAST report recommended that the structure of the IWGs/CGs be decoupled from the PCAs, but that change was not made.

However, in 2008 the first SSG was created. SSGs are not tied to budget reporting categories. Their members are at a higher level in their organizations than IWG and CG members, and usually have some budget authority. The SSG mechanism allows for increased flexibility and timeliness in forming interagency groups addressing areas of national priority.

The first SSG, also named CSIA, was formed in response to the 2008 Presidential Comprehensive National Cybersecurity Initiative (CNCI). It was joined in 2011 by the SSG for Health Information Technology R&D, chartered at the time that HHS ONC was developing a national strategy for health IT. The Wireless Spectrum Research and Development (WSRD) SSG was formed to advance the goals of the June 28, 2010 Presidential Memorandum: "Unleashing the Wireless Broadband Revolution."[18] The Big Data SSG

---

18. "Presidential Memorandum: Unleashing the Wireless Broadband Revolution." (June 28, 2010). The White House, Office of the Press Secretary. www.whitehouse.gov/the-press-office/presidential-memorandum-unleashing-wireless-broadband-revolution.

was formed in 2011 as OSTP was developing a National Big Data Initiative. An SSG for Cyber Physical Systems (CPS) was created in 2012.

SSGs are a significant and important addition to the NITRD coordination process—they engage in planning and coordination for important large emerging areas that span agencies. They are influential and visible as forums for agency discussion and as contact points for industry and academic engagement, and they have attracted new agency interest in NITRD.

> **Finding:** The SSGs introduced in recent years have strengthened the NITRD coordination function. The lower-level CGs have a more rigid structure that inhibits coordination of topics that cross PCA boundaries.
>
> **Recommendation 9:** NSTC and OSTP should strengthen the flexibility and responsiveness of the NITRD coordinating structure by continuing the use of SSGs, by decoupling the IWGs and CGs from the budget reporting structure, and by regularly reviewing the Group portfolio with an eye towards disbanding those Groups that have outlived their usefulness and starting others that reflect major changes in NIT R&D areas.

Agency Membership and Participation

As recommended, the number of NITRD agencies has increased. DHS, the Department of Energy Office of Electricity Delivery and Energy Reliability (DoE-EERE), DoT, the National Reconnaissance Office, and the Office of the National Coordinator for Health Information Technology (HHS-ONC) have joined; the Office of Nuclear Energy (DoE-ONE) has dropped out. Neither VHA nor the Centers for Disease Control (CDC) nor the Centers for Medicare and Medicaid Services (CMS) have joined, despite their potentially important roles in health IT; no part of DoEd has joined despite the growing interest in novel uses of IT for education at all levels. However, VHA is participating in the NITRD SSG on health IT, and the Office of Financial Research (OFR), a new agency in Treasury, participates in the Big Data SSG. Some agency personnel have suggested that the expected contribution to NCO funding is an inhibitor if advancing NIT is not central to the agency's mission.

> **Finding:** Agency membership in NITRD has increased, but there are still agencies missing whose participation would be valuable in advancing important national priorities.

Budget Matters

There were three recommendations in the 2010 report that were intended to create greater budget transparency, that is, to provide a better understanding of the government investment in NIT R&D, so that trends could be discerned, and so that future investment decisions could be informed by knowledge of current investment.

The first recommendation was that the joint Office of Management and Budget (OMB)/OSTP annual Science and Technology Budget Priority Memorandum reflect NITRD priorities. The NCO has been responsive to the recommendation that they keep OSTP informed of NITRD priorities, and the Memorandum for the 2014 Budget, although it is brief, does indeed state some of those priorities.

The second recommendation was that the NCO create a publicly available database of government-funded NIT research. The third recommendation was that the NCO and OMB redefine the budget reporting categories to separate NIT infrastructure for R&D in other fields from NIT R&D, and that they ensure more accurate reporting of both NIT infrastructure investment and NIT R&D investment. For a variety of reasons, those recommendations have proven to be more challenging.

Recall that there is no NITRD budget, per se. There is only a summary of NITRD-related portions of agency budgets (so-called cross-cuts), as categorized by the PCAs. The difficulty in providing a transparent summary of NITRD funding stems from the following issues:

1. Different agencies organize their budgets in different ways. In particular, many mission agencies structure their budgets in terms of tasks to satisfy their mission, not according to the disciplines and activities that contribute to mission goals. Since the agencies deal with different congressional authorization and appropriation committees, there are few reasons for uniform budget structuring across agencies, and little incentive to factor out NIT R&D.

2. In some agencies, the budgets of whole sub-organizations are classified as NITRD-related. For instance, the entire NSF Directorate for Computing and Information Science and Engineering (CISE) budget falls within NITRD, as does the entire DoE Advanced Scientific Computing Research (ASCR) budget. In other agencies, such as NIH or parts of DoD, there is an annual request to offices within an agency to report which budget components fall under NITRD PCAs. Inconsistencies arise among agencies or even from one year to the next in a given agency, because of differences in judgments of those doing the reporting.

3. High-end computing is the only NITRD area in which there is a distinction in the PCAs between infrastructure (HEC-I&A) and R&D (HEC-R&D). Representatives of other agencies assert that they are unable to separate infrastructure funding from funding for R&D.

4. In some instances, budget expenditures are not available in electronic form in a way that would facilitate the reporting of actual (as opposed to appropriated) investment in NIT R&D.

5. In cases where individual judgment determines inclusion in NITRD cross-cuts, there is an incentive to under-report NITRD funding, i.e. to interpret the PCAs narrowly. In contrast, it is in the NCO's interest to define reporting categories as broadly as possible, to increase the funding for their work.

As NIT R&D has both grown and broadened, it has been harder to assess the government investment in R&D that advances NIT because it is (inconsistently) conflated with investments in NIT infrastructure for uses other than NIT R&D. Infrastructure investments are important, and HPC infrastructure investments have been part of the coordination effort since 1991, but they are a distinct kind of investment. Distinguishing NIT R&D expenditures from infrastructure expenditures is not intended to diminish the importance of creating and supporting research infrastructure, which plays an essential role in R&D. Indeed, the 2010 PCAST report recommends increased infrastructure investment, particularly for testbeds that can be used for experimentation and evaluation of novel approaches to solving important problems. There are praiseworthy new projects to meet that need in areas such as networking and mobile health. However, infrastructure that uses conventional NIT to facilitate research in other disciplines is more a contributor to those disciplines than to furthering NIT. That distinction is not reflected in current NITRD budget reporting.

Finding: Transparent quantitative reporting of government investment in areas of NIT R&D is inhibited by longstanding agency reporting practices and by structuring of digital data that is inadequate for this task. Other means of evaluating the government's investment are needed.

Recommendation 10: OMB should continue its effort to digitize funding information and to enhance capabilities to create meaningful summary reports that cross agency boundaries.

Recommendation 11: OSTP, with guidance from PCAST, should develop a combination of quantitative and qualitative methods to assess the adequacy and appropriateness of government investments in NIT R&D.

V. Progress in 2010 Recommendations for Government Leadership

The 2010 report explains the profound importance of networking and information technology to the Nation's prosperity, its well-being, and its quality of life.[19] Maintaining the essential contributions of NIT to the Nation going forward depends on sustained advances in NIT R&D, and on the productive use of those advances for the national good. Achieving those advances and their uses depends on government leadership, both to ensure a skilled workforce and to ensure a sustained, healthy, and vibrant program of NIT R&D.

Education and Training

Both discovery and use of NIT advances requires an NIT-educated community of innovators, workers, and citizens. That education must start in childhood and continue for a lifetime. There are promising signs of increased attention to this need. The NSTC's Committee on STEM Education, which was created in response to the 2010 PCAST report on Education,[20] is off to a good start. NSF introduced a program in Computing Education for the 21st Century. Many of the mission agencies have created programs to educate more people in NIT topics essential to their missions. The CG for Social Economic and Workforce Implications of IT has created a subgroup on education. Yet, the states have been slow to introduce concepts of computer fluency in K-12[21] and higher education is not keeping up with the increasing demand for employees in computing occupations, as projected by the Bureau of Labor Statistics. [22]

> **Finding:** Both discovery and use of NIT advances requires an NIT-education community of innovators, workers, and citizens. The states have been slow to introduce concepts of computer fluency in K-12; higher education is not keeping up with the increasing demand for employees in computing occupations.
>
> **Recommendation 12:** The NSTC must continue to lead in bringing about the education of more children and adults in NIT, through the efforts of its Committee on STEM Education, in multi-agency programs to provide workers with skills in topics of importance to national priorities, and in the creation of opportunities for high-quality continuing education in NIT.

---

19. See footnote 2. Section 2.
20. President's Council of Advisors on Science and Technology. (2010). "Prepare and Inspire: K-12 Science, Technology, Engineering, and Math (STEM) Education for America's Future." Report to the President and Congress. www.whitehouse.gov/sites/default/files/microsites/ostp/pcast-stem-ed-final.pdf.
21. ACM and Computer Science Teachers Association. (2010). "Running on Empty: The Failure to Teach K–12 Computer Science in the Digital Age." www.acm.org/runningonempty/fullreport.pdf, Fig. 8. Computer fluency is "a robust understanding of what is needed to use information technology effectively across a broad range of applications." It is a stronger notion than computer literacy, which implies competency with computer applications such as word processing and e-mail. The term was introduced in "Being Fluent with Information Technology." National Academies Press. (1999).
22. Bureau of Labor Statistics 2010/2020 Employment Projections (Computing Occupations). Department of Labor. www.bls.gov/emp/ep_table_102.htm, http://www.bls.gov/emp/ep_table_112.htm.

Expert Strategic Guidance and Advice

The 2010 report also documents the essential role that Federal investment plays in NIT research and development, drawing on the conclusions of multiple well-respected studies.[23] The Federal Government must lead in ensuring that strong and sustained multi-agency R&D investments are made in NIT to address important national priorities. Among those priorities are the prosperity, health, and security of the Nation and its citizens.

The estimated $4B annual NIT R&D investments made by the Federal Government must be made wisely. As this report has documented, the Nation has in place a robust human infrastructure to coordinate the investments made by different agencies, limiting overlap, leveraging synergistic advances made in support of differing mission needs, and fueling the private sector.

But to continue to lead the world in the increasingly broad and rapidly changing domains of NIT, the Federal Government must also invest strategically, striking a balance between emerging and potentially transformative research and aspects of important core areas in which continued progress is essential. Insufficient attention to either new disruptive directions or the NIT base on which advances rest would weaken U.S. strength and leadership in NIT.

The challenges are daunting. The Nation's priorities in a range of areas, spanning transportation to health to national security, are sparking the need for NIT solutions of unprecedented technical ambition. At no time prior to the current era are we aware of such broad-based plans to implement "bleeding-edge" technologies, often at scales approaching that of the World-Wide Web. More often than not, the technologies being called for in real-world deployments are not "off the shelf," but must be invented as new technologies and then put immediately into practice. The potential benefits to quality of life are significant and transformational. But with such high technical ambition, often the design spaces that must be worked in are vast and consequently, the technical risks are enormous.

In this light, the problem of determining a national strategy for R&D investment requires the dedication of people at the highest levels of government, with the wisdom to appreciate new strategies and the ability to implement them in a sustained fashion. Their decisions must be informed by discipline-specific advice from the most knowledgeable experts in academia and the private sector.

The 2010 PCAST NITRD report recommended the establishment of a broad high-level standing committee of academic scientists, engineers, and industry leaders dedicated to providing sustained strategic advice in NIT. The reason PCAST cited for recommending that a *new* committee be formed was that no existing body had a combination of several characteristics that PCAST felt to be essential for this purpose. The rationale for a committee dedicated to NIT was the need for focus, so that important issues get timely and in-depth attention that combines scientific and technical considerations, policy considerations, and economic considerations. The motivation for a *standing* committee was the need for continuous attention so that advice would be proactive rather than reactive, allowing the committee to identify emerging issues early and incorporate them in a sustained strategic vision for the Nation's strength in NIT. PCAST also recommended that the standing committee be sufficiently large that its members

---

23. See footnote 2. Section 12.

have appropriate breadth and depth of knowledge and experience to provide a continuously evolving strategic vision. To date, such a standing committee has not been established, and there is still no other body with the above characteristics that meets the needs PCAST identified.

Since 2010, the need has only grown. We therefore recommend that PCAST itself form a standing subcommittee dedicated to this purpose, with an associated working group. The new working group would engage appropriate expertise from the NIT community and would operate on a regular and ongoing (as opposed to a project-specific) basis. The working group would survey the field and propose findings and recommendations, which PCAST could adopt in appropriate PCAST reports (including, but not limited to, the biennial NITRD program review). The standing subcommittee and working group we recommend would function in a manner analogous, in certain respects, to that of the very active and effective PCAST subcommittee and working group dedicated to advanced manufacturing.

Finding: In light of the broad impact of NIT and of its profound importance for the United States, the 2010 NITRD report recommended the creation of a sustained high-level standing committee to advise the Federal Government on both long-term and shorter-term strategy for NIT. There is still a pressing need for such a group.

Recommendation 13: The Federal Government must lead in continuing to ensure that strong multi-agency R&D investments are made in NIT to address important national priorities. PCAST should establish a high-level standing PCAST NIT subcommittee and associated high-level PCAST NIT working group, composed of expert academic scientists, engineers, and industry leaders who can provide sustained strategic advice.

Appendix A.
2010 PCAST Recommendations

INITIATIVES IN NIT R&D TO ACHIEVE AMERICA'S PRIORITIES

Recommendation 5-1: NIT for Health

The Federal Government, under the leadership of NSF and HHS, with participation from ONC, CMS, the Agency for Healthcare Research and Quality (AHRQ), NIST, VHA, DoD, and other interested agencies, should invest in a national, long-term, multi-agency research initiative on NIT for health that goes well beyond the current national program to adopt electronic health records. The initiative should include sponsorship of multi-disciplinary research on three themes:

- to make possible comprehensive lifelong multi-source health records for individuals;

- to enable both professionals and the public to obtain and act on health knowledge from diverse and varied sources as part of an interoperable health IT ecosystem; and

- to provide appropriate information, tools, and assistive technologies that empower individuals to take charge of their own health and healthcare and to reduce its cost.

Recommendation 5-2: NIT for Energy and Transportation

The Federal Government should invest in a national, long-term, multi-agency, multi-faceted research initiative on NIT for energy and transportation. As part of that initiative:

- DoE and NSF should be major sponsors of research for achieving dynamic power management in applications ranging from single devices to buildings to the power grid.

- NIST should organize the multi-stakeholder formulation of interoperable standards for real-time control. Interoperability facilitates repeated cycles of innovation by multiple vendors, promoting the development of versatile and robust NIT.

- DoD should continue to be a major sponsor of research on using NIT to achieve low-power systems and devices.

- DoT should sponsor ambitious NIT research relevant to surface and air transportation.

Recommendation 5-3: NIT for National and Homeland Security

The Federal Government should invest in a national, long-term, multi-agency research initiative on NIT that assures both the security and the robustness of cyber-infrastructure. NSF and DoD, in collaboration DHS, should aggressively accelerate funding and coordination of fundamental research:

- to discover more effective ways to build trustworthy computing and communications systems;

- to continue to develop new NIT defense mechanisms for today's infrastructure, and most importantly;

- to develop fundamentally new approaches for the design of the underlying architecture of our cyber-infrastructure so that it can be made truly resilient to cyber-attack, natural disaster, and inadvertent failure.

Recommendation 5-4: NIT for Education—NIT R&D on Educational Technologies

DoEd, in collaboration with NSF, should provide robust and diversified support for fundamental NIT R&D that will lay the foundation for educational technologies such as personalized electronic tutors, serious games and interactive environments for education, and mobile and social education technologies. The support for NIT-based education should extend from pre-school settings to lifelong learning.

Recommendation 5-5: NIT for Education—Evaluation of Educational Technologies

DoEd, in collaboration with NSF, should have a long-term program to evaluate promising technology coming out of the research community in trials that include large numbers of sites and participants. Technology that proves its worth should be transferred into the schools. This program will require evolution of curricula and school processes and procedures.

Recommendation 5-6: NIT for Digital Democracy

NSTC should lead a multi-agency effort to define infrastructure, tools, and best practices that will increase the opportunities for digital democracy at all levels of government. Both the NIT research community and representatives of the public at large should participate in the planning process. The plan should have an emphasize on using the results of fundamental research in NIT to enable more efficient government and to improve the quantity and quality of information and ideas flowing into, out of, and within government. It should create pathways for fundamental research to be explored and evaluated on national testbeds, and for high impact approaches to be translated into practice.

INVESTMENTS IN THE NIT RESEARCH FRONTIERS

The Federal Government must increase investment in those fundamental NIT research frontiers that will accelerate progress across a broad range of priorities. Among such investments:

Recommendation 7-1: Privacy and Confidentiality

NSF and DARPA, with the participation of other relevant agencies, should invest in a broad, multi-agency research program on the fundamentals of privacy protection and protected disclosure of confidential data. Privacy and confidentiality concerns arise in virtually all uses of NIT.

Recommendation 7-2: NIT and People

NSF, DARPA, and HHS should create a collaborative research program that augments the study of individual human-computer interaction with a comprehensive investigation to understand and advance human-machine and social collaboration and problem-solving in a networked, on-line environment where large numbers of people participate in common activities. Understanding such collective human-NIT interactions is increasingly important for defense, for health, and for the activities of daily life.

Recommendation 7-3: Large-Scale Data Management and Analysis

NSF should expand its support for fundamental research in data collection, storage, management, and automated large-scale analysis based on modeling and machine learning. The ever-increasing use of computers, sensors, and other digital devices is generating huge amounts of digital data, making it a pervasive NIT-enabled asset. In collaboration with NIT researchers, every agency should support research, to apply the best known methods and to develop new approaches and new techniques to address data-rich problems that arise in its mission domain. Agencies should ensure access to and retention of critical community research data collections.

Recommendation 7-4: NIT and the Physical World

NSF and DARPA, in collaboration with those agencies tackling problems whose solution entails instrumenting the physical world—including the EPA, DoE, DoT, other parts of DoD, NIH, USDA, and NOAA—should increase research in advanced domain-specific sensors, integration of NIT into physical systems, and innovative robotics in order to enhance NIT-enabled interaction with the physical world.

Recommendation 7-5: Continued Investment in NIT R&D Core Areas and Sustainment of Research Infrastructure

New investments must not supplant continued investment in important core areas in which government-funded research is advancing. Continued attention must also be given to sustained high-quality shared research infrastructure, including new forms of infrastructure to support new research areas and paradigms.

Recommendation 7-6: Scalable Systems and Networking—Core Research

NSF, DARPA, and other organizations should continue their leadership and funding of core research into scalable systems in order to ensure that networked systems will adapt to the ever-changing needs of applications, to the capabilities engendered by new technology, and to evolving needs for security and privacy.

Recommendation 7-7: Scalable Systems and Networking—Open Systems

To foster an innovative ecosystem in NIT, government agencies concerned with networked systems operations, including DoD, NSF, and FCC, must continue to encourage and invest in open systems development. They must coordinate with standards organizations (IETF, W3C) and the NIT industry to ensure that standards pertaining to the different interfaces within and among the layers of the networked systems environment are defined and kept up to date.

Recommendation 7-8: Scalable Systems and Networking—Wireless Systems

In the area of wireless systems, NSF, FCC, and NTIA should partner to create, sustain, and promote the use of a nationwide infrastructure for spectrum monitoring that cuts across commercial, public safety

DESIGNING A DIGITAL FUTURE: FEDERALLY FUNDED RESEARCH AND DEVELOPMENT IN
NETWORKING AND INFORMATION TECHNOLOGY

and DoD applications. NSF, DHS, and NTIA should partner to create programs that promote innovative use of public safety frequencies. NSF, DHS, and DARPA should jointly articulate the synergies among their individual needs and programs in wireless spectrum management.

Recommendation 7-9: Software Creation and Evolution

NSF, DARPA, and other organizations that need software tailored to their mission requirements should continue their leadership and funding of core research in methods to improve the design, development, modification, and maintenance of all varieties of software. That research should address language design, tools, analysis methods, methods for collaborative design and development, and techniques that provide security and robustness. Attention must be given to system design and programming for scalability, paradigms for parallelism at multiple levels of granularity, software for heterogeneous systems involving interaction with the physical world, and software for systems that incorporate human interaction. Long term evaluative research is required to determine which tools and techniques yield sustainable improvement in software creation.

Recommendation 7-10: High-Performance Computing

NSF, DARPA, and DoE should invest in a coordinated program of basic research on architectures, algorithms, and software for next-generation HPC systems. Such research should not be limited to the acceleration of traditional applications, but should include work on systems capable of (a) efficiently analyzing vast quantities of both numerical and non-numerical data, (b) handling problems requiring real-time response, and (c) accelerating new applications. Specific areas of investigation should include:

- Novel system architectures for massively parallel computing
- High-bandwidth, low-latency processor interconnection networks
- Reliability and fault-tolerance in massively parallel computer systems
- Hardware and software design techniques for the dramatic reduction of power consumption
- Data-intensive computing, including non-numerical applications
- Programming models and languages for massively parallel machines
- Systems software for massively parallel systems
- Improved approaches for system management

In addition to designing next-generation systems, significant effort must be devoted to R&D focused on extracting the greatest possible scientific benefit from current leading-edge systems.

TECHNOLOGICAL AND HUMAN RESOURCES

Recommendation 9-1: Education and Human Resources

The NSTC's Committee on STEM Education proposed in a recent PCAST report must exercise strong leadership to bring about fundamental changes in K-12 STEM education in the United States, among them the incorporation of computer science as an essential component.

NITRD COORDINATION PROCESS AND STRUCTURE

Recommendation 11-1: Government Coordination of NIT R&D

The effectiveness of government coordination of NIT R&D should be enhanced:

- The number of NITRD member agencies should be increased. The duration, management levels, and topic areas of the NITRD coordinating groups should be flexible. Budget reporting categories should be decoupled from the coordinating structure.

- The NCO for NITRD should create a publicly available database of government-funded NIT research, and should provide regular detailed reporting to the Director of OSTP.

- OMB and OSTP should reflect NITRD priorities in their annual Budget Priority Memorandum.

Recommendation 11-2: Budget Reporting Categories

The NCO and OMB should redefine the budget reporting categories to separate NIT infrastructure for R&D in other fields from NIT R&D, and should ensure more accurate reporting of both NIT infrastructure investment and NIT R&D investment.

Recommendation 11-3: Federal Government Leadership

The Federal Government must lead in ensuring that strong multi-agency R&D investments are made in NIT to address important national priorities.

- OSTP should establish a broad, high-level standing committee of academic scientists, engineers, and industry leaders dedicated to providing sustained strategic advice in NIT.

The NSTC should lead in defining and promoting the major NIT research initiatives that are required to achieve the most important existing and emerging national priorities.

Appendix B.
Additional Experts Providing Input

Byron Barker
Chief, Strategic Planning Division
Office of Spectrum Management
National Telecommunications and Information
Administration

Francine Berman
Professor of Computer Science
Rensselaer Polytechnic Institute

Brian Biegel
Acting Deputy Chief of the NASA Advanced
Supercomputing Division
National Aeronautics and Space Administration

Alan Blatecky
Director
Office of Cyberinfrastructure
National Science Foundation

Robert Bohn
Cloud Computing Program Manager
National Institute of Standards and Technology

Steven Brobst
Chief Technology Officer
Teradata

Randal Bryant
Dean
School of Computer Science
Carnegie Mellon University

Andrew Clegg
Program Director
Directorate for Mathematical and Physical
Sciences (MPS)
National Science Foundation

Mark Dean
Chief Technology Office
IBM Middle East and Africa
IBM Research

Deborah Estrin
Professor of Computer Science
Professor of Electrical Engineering
University of California, Los Angeles

Edward Felten
Director, Center for Information Technology
Policy; Professor of Computer Science and Public
Affairs
Princeton University
Chief Technologist
Federal Trade Commission

Douglas Fridsma
Director
Office of Standards and Interoperability
Department of Health and Human Services

Deborah Frincke
Deputy Director
Research Directorate
National Security Agency

Robert Gold
Director, Information Systems and Cyber Security
Office of the Assistant Secretary for Defense
Department of Defense

William Gropp
Paul and Cynthia Saylor Professor of Computer
Science University of Illinois, Urbana-Champaign

Daniel Hitchcock
Associate Director
Office of Advanced Scientific Computing
Research
Office of Science
Department of Energy

Suzanne Iacono
Senior Science Advisor
Directorate for Computer and Information
Science & Engineering
National Science Foundation

Farnam Jahanian
Assistant Director
Computer and Information Science &
Engineering
National Science Foundation

David Jakubek
Deputy Director
Information Systems
Office of the Secretary of Defense
Department of Defense

Anita Jones
Professor Emerita
University of Virginia

Dan Kaufman
Director
Information Innovation Office
Defense Advanced Research Projects Agency
Department of Defense

Dai H. Kim
Associate Director for Advanced Computing
Information Systems and Cyber Security
Office of the Assistant Secretary for Defense
Department of Defense

Ed Lazowska
Bill & Melinda Gates Chair in Computer
Science and Engineering
University of Washington

Herbert Lin
Chief Scientist
Computer Science and Telecommunications
Board
National Research Council

Mark Luker
Associate Director
National Coordination Office for Networking
and Information Technology Research and
Development

Peter Lyster
Program Director
Division of Biomedical Technology,
Bioinformatics, and Computational Biology
National Institutes of Health

Douglas Maughan
Division Director
Cyber Security R&D Branch, Science and
Technology Directorate
Department of Homeland Security

Michael May
Associate Director for Software Technologies
Assistant Secretary for Defense
Department of Defense

Ernest McDuffie
Lead of the National Initiative for Cybersecurity
Education
National Institute of Standards and Technology

Andrea Norris
Director of Center for Information Technology
(CIT) and the Chief Information Officer (CIO)
National Institutes of Health

Todd Park
U.S. Chief Technology Officer and Assistant to the
President
Chief Technology Officer
Office of Science and Technology Policy

Kamie Roberts
Associate Director for Federal & Industrial
Relations
National Institute of Standards and Technology

Charles Romine
Director, Information Technology Laboratory
National Institute of Standards and Technology

Douglas Rosendale
Senior Physician Advisor/Clinical Informatics/
Office of Health Information
Department of Veterans Affairs

Fred Schneider
Samuel B. Eckert Professor of Computer Science.
Department of Computer Science
Cornell University

Robert Sproull
Vice President and Fellow
Sun Microsystems

George Strawn
Director, National Coordination Office for
Networking and Information Technology
Research and Development

Steven VanRoekel
Federal Chief Information Officer and
Administrator
Office of Electronic Government
Office of Management and Budget

Appendix C. Acknowledgments

Jonathan Agre
Research Staff Member
Institute for Defense Analyses

Kaitlin Bernell
Student Volunteer
Office of Science and Technology Policy

Genevieve Croft
Student Volunteer
Office of Science and Technology Policy

Pat Falcone
Associate Director for National Security and
International Affairs
Office of Science and Technology Policy

Karen Gordon
Research Staff Member
Institute for Defense Analyses

Nayanee Gupta
Research Staff Member
IDA Science and Technology Policy Institute

Tom Kalil
Deputy Director for Policy
Office of Science and Technology Policy

Bhavya Lal
Research Staff Member
IDA Science and Technology Policy Institute

Sarah Nash
Research Staff Member
IDA Science and Technology Policy Institute

Deborah Stine
Professor of Practice
Carnegie Mellon University
Past Executive Director, PCAST

Richmond Wong
Student Volunteer
Office of Science and Technology Policy

Appendix D. Acronyms

ARPA-ED	Advanced Research Projects Agency for Education
ASCR	Advanced Scientific Computing Research
CDC	Centers for Disease Control
CMS	Centers for Medicare and Medicaid Services
CNCI	Comprehensive National Cybersecurity Initiative
CISE	Computing and Information Science and Engineering
CG	Coordinating Group
CPS	Cyber Physical Systems
CSIA	Cyber Security and Information Assurance
DARPA	Defense Advanced Research Project Agency
DREN	Defense Research and Engineering Network
DoD	Department of Defense
DoE	Department of Energy
DoE-EERE	Department of Energy Office of Electricity Delivery and Energy Reliability
DHS	Department of Homeland Security
DoT	Department of Transportation
ESnet	Energy Sciences Network
EARS	Enhancing Access to Radio Spectrum
EPA	Environmental Protection Agency
FCC	Federal Communication Commission
FLOPS	Floating point operations per second
GENI	Global Environment for Network Innovations
GDP	Gross domestic product
HCSS	High Confidence Software and Systems
HITIDE	Health Information Technology Innovation and Development Environments
HITRD	Health Information Technology Research and Development
HEC	High End Computing
HPC	High-performance computing
IWG	Interagency Working Group
ICES	Interface between Computer Science and Economics & Social Sciences
MOOC	Massive open online course
NASA	National Aeronautics and Space Administration
ONC	Office of the National Coordinator for Health Information Technology
NIST	National Institute of Standards and Technology

NIH	National Institutes of Health
NOAA	National Oceanic and Atmospheric Administration
NSF	National Science Foundation
NSA	National Security Agency
NTIA	National Telecommunications and Information Administration
NIT	Networking and Information Technology
NITRD	Networking and Information Technology Research and Development
OFR	Office of Financial Research
OMB	Office of Management and Budget
DoE-ONE	Office of Nuclear Energy
OSTP	Office of Science and Technology Policy
PITAC	President's Information Technology Advisory Committee
PCA	Program Component Area
R&D	Research and Development
SDAV	Scalable Data Management, Analysis and Visualization
SEES	Science, Engineering, and Education for Sustainability
STEM	Science, Technology, Engineering, and Mathematics
SSG	Senior Steering Group
SoCS	Social-Computational Systems
SCORE	Special Cyber Operations Research and Engineering
SHARP	Strategic Health IT Advanced Research Projects
NCO	National Coordinating Office
NSTC	National Science and Technology Council
VHA	Veterans Health Administration
USDA	U.S. Department of Agriculture
HHS	U.S. Department of Health and Human Services
USGS	U.S. Geological Survey
WSRD	Wireless Spectrum Research and Development

President's Council of Advisors on Science and
Technology (PCAST)

www.whitehouse.gov/ostp/pcast

www.ingramcontent.com/pod-product-compliance
Lightning Source LLC
LaVergne TN
LVHW060148070326

832902LV00018B/3010